BOBBY & MANDEE'S

T0014276

Street Smarts

How to Be a Safe Pedestrian

Hey, parents! Read this book with your kids!

Always be aware when you're walking!

CHILDREN'S SAFETY BOOK

Robert Kahn

with illustrations by Lynda Farrington Wilson

Bobby & Mandee's Street Smarts: How to Be a Safe Pedestrian

All marketing and publishing rights guaranteed to and reserved by:

FUTURE HORIZONS

817·277·0727 | Fax: 817·277·2270
www.FHautism.com | info@FHautism.com

© 2023 Robert Kahn
Illustrations © 2023 Lynda Farrington Wilson
All rights reserved.

No part of this product may be reproduced in any manner whatsoever without written permission of Future Horizons, except in the case of brief quotations embodied in reviews.

ISBN: 9781957984261

DEDICATION

I wish to thank my family and friends for all of their

support with this book.

Hello again, I'm Bobby, and you remember my sister, Mandee.

In this book, we are going to talk about being safe when you are a pedestrian and crossing a street.

Who is a pedestrian, you ask?
A pedestrian is anyone who is walking
outside on a path or a street.

Mandee, did you know many pedestrians are hurt every year? Today we are going to talk about safety tips to keep in mind when you are a pedestrian.

Let's go for a walk. We will go over the safety tips as we practice them, especially at intersections where there are crosswalks.

We will leave our driveway and walk down our street. Mandee, always stay on the sidewalk and walk the same way that traffic is traveling.

If there isn't a sidewalk, walk facing traffic and as far away from cars as possible.

As we continue walking, Mandee, let's talk about intersections. There are two kinds of intersections.

two

2

The first one is called an uncontrolled intersection.

An uncontrolled intersection doesn't have
any signs or signals, and people have to
give each other the right of way.

Pedestrians always have the right of way, but make sure you're careful before you cross the street, and make sure the driver sees you.

The second one is a controlled intersection. A controlled intersection has signs that tell drivers what to do. It will usually have a stop sign on the corners, and drivers should obey the signs. Or the intersection will have a traffic signal.

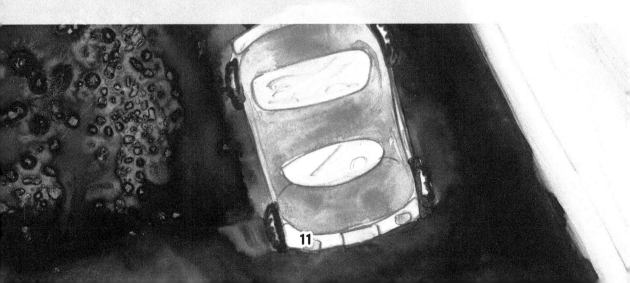

Mandee, let's continue our walk to the intersection at the end of our street. It is an unmarked intersection, so we have to remember what to do.

12

Bobby, sometimes I see people walking and they aren't paying attention to where they are going or they are doing something with their cell phone and not looking at what's around them.

Yes, Mandee, those are not good things to be doing. Someone can walk into things or even fall off of the sidewalk if they aren't paying attention when they are walking.

If kids need to use a cell phone, teach them to stop walking and find a safe area to talk.

Remember: always walk carefully and be ready for anything that may happen. Be sure you know what's going on around you, and don't allow your vision to be blocked by hats, clothing, or items that you are carrying.

Oh look, Bobby, we're coming up to
our first intersection.

Yes, we are, Mandee.
Tell me the safety tips before we cross.

Pedestrians need to be especially careful at intersections. Drivers may fail to yield the right-of-way to pedestrians while turning onto another street.

Always make sure you are seen.
You can do this by making eye contact
with drivers when crossing busy streets.

If you're walking at night, wear bright colors or reflective clothing. Also, carry a flashlight when walking in the dark.

Before we cross, we will look to our left (1), then to our right (2), and then to our left again (3) before we start to cross the street.

We will continue looking until we safely cross the street. This is to make sure that a car isn't coming and to be sure we safely get across the street.

Bobby, we have to make sure that there isn't a car turning into the street. Also, we must be aware if a car is backing up and to make sure they see us.

Bobby, also never dart or run out into an intersection. Also don't cross between parked cars.

This is important wherever you are walking on a street.

Another important thing to remember is that children under ten years old need to cross the street with a trusted adult.

Each child is unique, but children under ten are unable to judge the speed and distance of an oncoming car.

Mandee, that was very well done, great job. Let's continue our walk to the next intersection, which is a controlled one.

Well, here we are; this is a busy intersection. This intersection has a pedestrian signal.

Watch the pedestrian signal, not the traffic signal, and follow the "WALK/DON'T WALK" lights (they are set up to help you cross safely). Also, look for pedestrian push buttons for crossing protection at these intersections.

Also, if there are audible instructions saying to cross the intersection, be sure to look both ways before and while you are crossing the intersection.

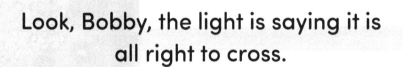
Look, Bobby, the light is saying it is all right to cross.

Remember, Bobby, we have to look to our left, then to our right, and then to our left again before we start to cross the street.

And again, we will continue looking
until we safely cross the street. This is to
make sure that a car isn't coming and to
be sure we safely get across the street.

Again, Mandee, you did an excellent job remembering everything to do to be safe.

Let's go inside this mini-market and buy something cold to drink before we start our walk home.

Bobby and Mandee's Pedestrian Test

1. Who is a pedestrian? (answer on page 3)

2. You walk which way when you're walking on a sidewalk when there is traffic? (answer on page 6)

3. You walk which way when there isn't a sidewalk when there is traffic? (answer on page 7)

4. What is an uncontrolled intersection? (answer on page 9)

5. What is a controlled intersection? (answer on page 11)

6. Is it all right for people to be walking and not paying attention or doing something with their cell phone and not looking at what's around them? (answer on page 15)

7. What is a good way to make sure you are seen by drivers? (answer on page 18)

8. If you are walking at night, what are some ways to make sure you are noticed? (answer on page 19)

9. When you are about to cross an intersection, how do you look for cars? (answer on page 20)

10. When you are crossing the street, what should you do? (answer on page 21)

11. Should you run into the street or cross between parked cars? (answer on page 23)

12. What is a pedestrian signal? (answer on page 26)

Printed in the USA
CPSIA information can be obtained
at www.ICGtesting.com
JSHW071948110823
46385JS00002B/2

9 781957 984261